COLT
Horse

PUGGLE
Platypus

Elephant

Giraffe

Camel

Whale

Hippopotamus

CALVES

Cow

TADPOLES or POLLYWOGS
Frog or Toad

OWLET
Owl

The story you are about to read is mostly true.
No animal names have been changed.
Please note, baby sea otters and raccoons can also
be called kits, and baby horses are called foals—
a male is a colt and a female is a filly.
The characters in this book have requested this clarification.

For Laura, Andy, and Ben, who were all born babies
and grew into supercool humans —MF

For Jess —BJS

I Was Born a Baby
Text copyright © 2022 by Meg Fleming
Illustrations copyright © 2022 by Brandon James Scott
All rights reserved. Printed in the United States of America.
No part of this book may be used or reproduced in any manner whatsoever without
written permission except in the case of brief quotations embodied in critical articles
and reviews. For information address HarperCollins Children's Books, a division of
HarperCollins Publishers, 195 Broadway, New York, NY 10007.
www.harpercollinschildrens.com

Library of Congress Control Number: 2021939627
ISBN 978-0-06-315721-7

The artist used Adobe Photoshop to create the digital illustrations for this book.
Typography by Chelsea C. Donaldson
22 23 24 25 26 PC 10 9 8 7 6 5 4 3 2
❖
First Edition

I WAS BORN A BABY

WRITTEN BY **Meg Fleming**

PICTURES BY **Brandon James Scott**

HARPER

An Imprint of HarperCollinsPublishers

I was born a baby.

I was born a colt.

I was born a piglet.

I'm a billy goat.

I was born a fawn.

I was born a kit.

I was born a little lamb.

I was born a chick.

No way, no how!
That can't be true!

I'm a chick, too!

I was born a hatchling
and fluffed into a duckling.

I grew into a gosling.

I puffed into a puffling!

I was born to giggle.

I was born to laugh.

I was born to *super*-glide!

I was born a calf.

No way, no how!
That can't be true!

I'm a calf!

I'm a calf!

I'm a calf, too!

I was born to store.

I was born to snuggle.

I was born a porcupette.

I was born a puggle?

I was born to spray.

I was born to scrub.

I was born an owlet.

I was born a cub.

No way, no how!
That can't be true!

I'm a cub!

I was born a joey.

I'm a joey, too.

I was *also* born a joe.

I'm a kangaroo.

I was born a kitten.

I'm a little guppy.

I'm a little pup,
but people call me puppy.

No way, no how!
That can't be true!

I'm a pup!

I'm a pup!

I'm a pup, too!

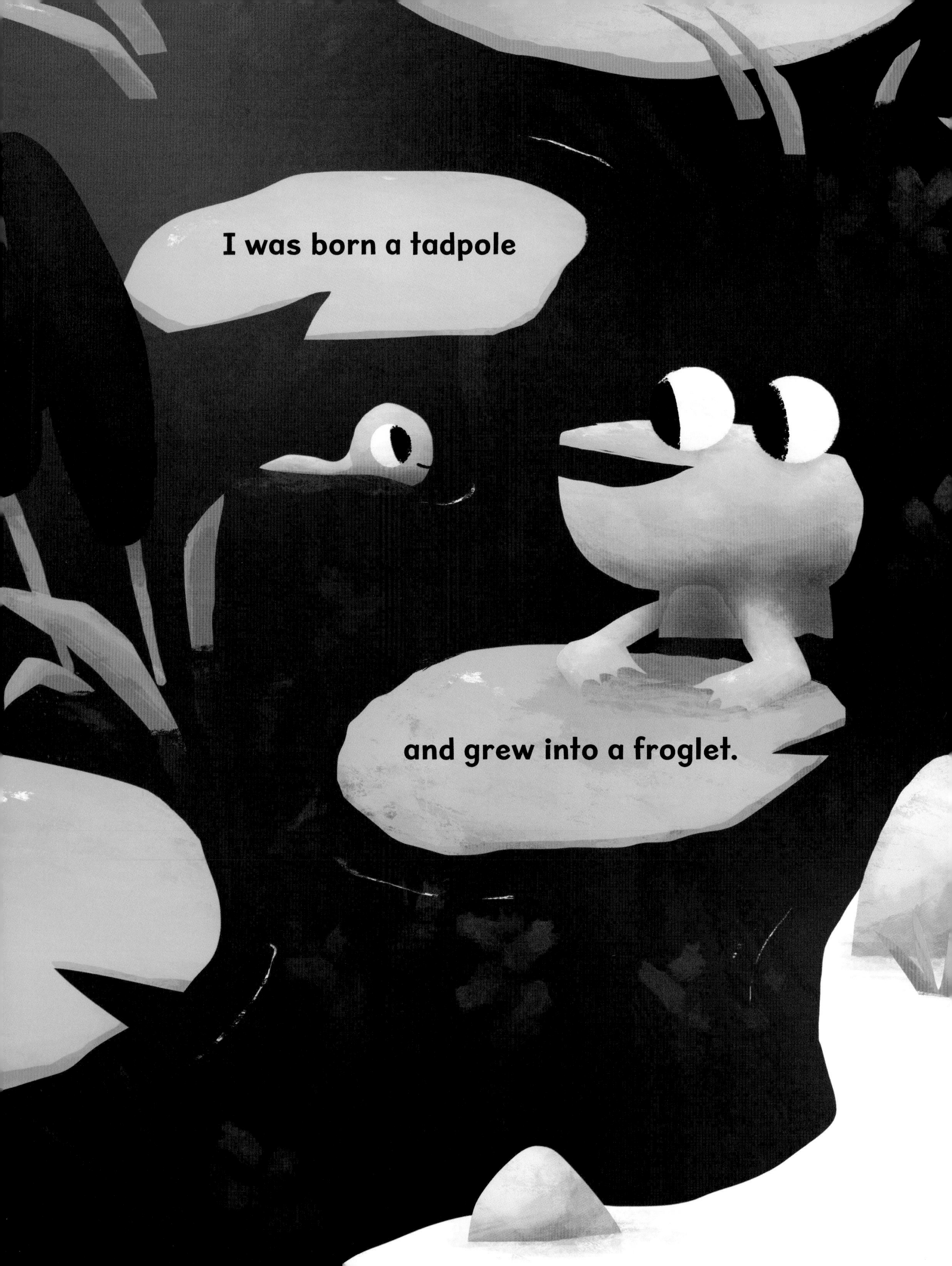
I was born a tadpole
and grew into a froglet.

I grew into a toadlet.

I was born a hoglet.

I was born a larva
   and grew into a squid.

I was born a baby
and grew into a kid!

Me *four* . . .
it's true!

I'm a kid!

YOU'RE

A KID!

I'm a kid, too.

Tiger

Walrus

LARVA
Squid

Bear

Hyena

Raccoon

Lion

CUBS

Opossum

Kangaroo

LAMB
Sheep

Koala

Wombat

JOEYS